Solitary Witchcraft for Beginners

Immersive Magic, Volume 2

Merryl Kowalska

Published by Merryl Kowalska, 2022.

While every precaution has been taken in the preparation of this book, the publisher assumes no responsibility for errors or omissions, or for damages resulting from the use of the information contained herein.

SOLITARY WITCHCRAFT FOR BEGINNERS

First edition. December 8, 2022.

Copyright © 2022 Merryl Kowalska.

ISBN: 979-8215524282

Written by Merryl Kowalska.

Also by Merryl Kowalska

Immersive Magic
A Guide to Acquiring an Astral Magic Wand
Solitary Witchcraft for Beginners

Table of Contents

Introduction 1

Understanding Solitary Witchcraft 3

The Mind of a Magus 5

Meditation 7

Magical Energy 11

Energy Breathing Technique 13

Energy Quality 15

The Elements 17

Get to Know the Elements 21

Touch the Earth 23

Energy Ball 25

Programming Your Energy Ball 27

Bubble Shield 29

Mental Projection 31

Dancing Flame 35

Inner Light Meditation 37

Magical Health 39

Drawing Down the Moon 41

Magical Bath 43

Wish Bird 45

Best Practices 47

A Call to Christ...51

For Olivia

Introduction

Immersive Magic: Solitary Witchcraft for Beginners is an occult codex that teaches the ways of magic. It is written for new magical practitioners and those who want to start on a magical journey. It is also designed for solitary practice, which means that you can actually start experiencing a magical life completely on your own and without any external help. Hence, nothing can stop you.

Immersive Magic: Solitary Witchcraft for Beginners reveals the essential teachings and practices of witchcraft. It is also written in a simple, direct, and easy-to-understand format, so that you can easily focus on learning and experiencing the magical life. This book will initiate you into the art of witchcraft. You will learn the right ancient knowledge, and you will be equipped with the right practices, so that you can truly experience what it truly means to live a magical life, and not just know it on an intellectual level. After all, true witchcraft is meant to be lived and experienced on a deep and personal level.

Another benefit of solitary witchcraft is that you do not need to follow rules that you do not like. You can enjoy so much more freedom and even exercise your creativity. It will not force you to do these that you would rather not engage in. Indeed, if you are looking for a magical and spiritual path that will allow you to enjoy so much freedom, then you would not go wrong with the solitary witchcraft approach.

It should be noted that solitary witchcraft does not mean that you are completely alone. Once you reach a deeper understanding of the universe, you will realize that you are, in fact, never alone. The energy of the universe keeps on flowing, and you are actually one with all things. Solitary witchcraft is not about being alone, but it is simply not being part of a formal and strict group or tradition. It is about being free and being who you truly are. It is about self-expression and absolute exercise of freewill. It is also about wonder and art. Indeed, there is so much that this path has to offer, but the question is: Are you ready for it? Do you have the courage to walk where angels fear to tread?

If you feel an inner voice or calling within you, or if you feel a desire within for magic and spirituality, then come, and we shall take this path together, to behold and embrace the path of solitary witchcraft.

Understanding Solitary Witchcraft

Solitary witchcraft is the form of witchcraft that is practiced without being included in a group or coven. It is something that you can do all by yourself; hence, it is *solitary*. It is magic in and of itself. In fact, it is a very intimate form of magic. It is also a recommended path to self-discovery and spiritual enlightenment.

There are many ways to define what witchcraft is. Witchcraft is as meaningful as you make it. For our own purposes, we shall treat witchcraft and magic as one and the same with a view that witchcraft is the magical-spiritual practice that elevates the soul and connects us to the Divine, as well as the art of causing change in the universe for the manifestation of your will.

Unlike other witchcraft traditions, solitary witchcraft does not impose any rules. You are free to exercise your magic in any way that you want. However, this does not mean that you can just abuse your powers. You are still free to do so, but you must also be aware of the consequences in accordance with universal laws.

Solitary witchcraft is more like a form than a particular name by which you shall call your practice. In fact, you are free to call your practice in any way that you want. After all, what is more important than the name is the things that you actually do (and do not do).

Eclectic practitioners of magic are also under the umbrella term of *solitary witchcraft*. Sadly, many eclectic practitioners these days are quite irresponsible and lazy. They do not even realize what witchcraft is really all about. It is a disgrace to even consider them as true practitioners of the magical arts.

The path that this book offers is much more sincere and intimate, and it is a path that leads to many other paths — and you have absolute freedom to choose wherever you want to go.

A true solitary witchcraft practitioner is not someone who is lost in the world not knowing what to do. But rather, they are those who are deeply engaged in magical study and practice — and here is an important thing: you ought to be living and experiencing a real magical life daily.

In solitary witchcraft, you are free to choose the branch of magic that you would like to specialize in. After all, the rules and principles of magic are always connected. Just as there is oneness of spirituality, there is also oneness of magical practices.

Last but not least, solitary witchcraft is a personal craft, so much so that once you really engage in it, there is no way that you will ever be the same again.

The Mind of a Magus

It is a well-established principle in occult science that all true and most genuine magic starts and ends in the mind. All forms of magic have one common point and source, and that is the mind.

If you really want to have any real progress in the magical arts, then you must train your mind. Actually, it is not the mind itself that needs training, but it is about removing all the blockages that you have created against it. The mind is already a powerful source of magic. However, much of the modern world has restricted the mind. In fact, so many people these days are not even aware of the true powers of their mind. In witchcraft, we go beyond the ordinary and all these limitations, and we rise above so that we can have a taste of divinity and real magic.

This is actually not difficult to do as long as you know how to do it. This is where the practice of witchcraft comes in, especially the practice of solitary witchcraft.

Never forget that your mind is your most powerful weapon. To unleash the true powers of the mind, you must live the magical life. The practice of meditation is also strongly recommended.

But how does the mind become so powerful? What makes it so magically effective? The key lies in the universal principles that all things are of the mind, and that your mind is always connected to the Divine Mind, The Creator of All Things. As such, you are never alone for the Divine works in you and through you. Remember: Any real spiritual progress is always a step closer to Divinity.

It must be clarified that your mind is already very powerful as it is right now. But, just to make it clear, there is the lower mind and the higher mind. The higher mind is what we are referring to when we say that it is already powerful, and it is also the mind that is used in magical work. The lower mind is the part of the mind that deals with mundane stuff, and it only has a simple and small role to play in magical work. The key is to be able to free the higher mind as much as you could by taking down the walls that you have built against it, such as lack of faith, wrong views, lack of willpower, and so on.

You must understand that for magic to work, the mind must be ready for it. This is the reason why those without magical training will never be able to do the things that a practitioner can do even though they follow the steps or instructions by the very letter. It is because their minds have so many walls and clouds that they could not unleash real magical powers.

The mind of a true magus has to be peaceful and serene. It should be noted that you will be more able to harness magical energy when the mind is calm and quiet. So, learn to free the mind, and you will surely be able to enjoy great magical powers and benefits.

Meditation

When it comes to quieting and freeing the mind, regular practice of meditation is highly encouraged. In fact, many practitioners agree that if you really want any real progress in the magical arts, then regular practice of meditation is an absolute requirement.

There are countless meditation techniques that have been developed through the years, but you do not need to learn all of them. In fact, learning a single meditation technique would be fine. The important thing is not to learn different techniques, but to learn a meditation technique and practice it regularly. In fact, even the most basic breathing meditation would be fine, and it will do wonders.

In our modern time, people see meditation as nothing more than a way to relax the mind and destress. However, it should be noted that meditation started as a spiritual practice, and it will always be a spiritual practice. Relaxing the mind and being able to destress are just some of the amazing benefits of practicing meditation regularly.

Never forget that meditation is, first and foremost, a spiritual practice. It is also an effective and natural way to develop your overall psychic faculties.

There are people who feel intimidated when they encounter the word *meditation*. It should be clarified that meditation is very easy to do. It is so easy and simple that it is more about not doing anything than having to do something. Anyone can meditate, but the problem is that only a few actually make time to meditate. If you are a magical practitioner, then you must prioritize the practice of meditation by making time for it. Having said that, let us now go to the actual meditation proper.

The meditation technique that you are about to learn is known as *breathing meditation.* It is the simplest form of meditation, and yet it is one of the most powerful meditation techniques. Many masters and seekers have practiced this meditation for many years. In fact, even the Buddha also practiced this meditation. Having said that, the steps are as follows:

Be comfortable and relax. Close your eyes and free the mind. Do not think about anything. Now is the time for meditation, and this is not the time to think.

Breathe through your nose. With eyes closed, gently focus on your breathing. If thoughts appear in the mind, ignore them, and only focus on your breath. Breath is life. Anyone who meditates on the breath meditates on life.

Breathe and let go. Be one with your breath. Be the breath. Become life.

At any time that you want to end this meditation, simply bring your awareness back to your physical body, slowly move your fingers and toes, and very gently open your eyes with a smile.

A good meditation is always simple and direct. The more complicated a meditation technique is, the harder it will be for the mind to become quiet and still, and this is what makes the breathing meditation very effective. Indeed, regular practice of the said meditation will significantly develop your overall spiritual and magical faculties.

If nothing seems to happen on your first attempts, do not be discouraged. Just keep practicing daily. The more that you practice, the more that you will improve and access a deeper state of mind and being.

A basic rule in magic is to meditate at least twice daily. If you can meditate more than twice a day, then that would even be better.

What about the length of time that you should spend in meditation? In meditation, time is not that important. The reason for this is that once you access a deep state of mind and being, time shall cease to exist. This explains how advanced meditators are able to spend long hours in meditation without being bothered. Hence, instead of focusing on the time that you spend meditating, you should focus more on having a good-quality meditation experience.

Take note of this: If you really want any real progress in your magical life, regular practice of meditation is definitely a must. You might not appreciate it in the beginning; but if you just keep practicing it, you will surely be very glad for doing it soon.

Magical Energy

If you have been studying the magical arts for some time now, you will definitely encounter the term *magical energy* or simply *energy*. This refers to the energy of magic, which is the energy that pervades the whole universe and all the cosmos. It is inside you and all around you. Everything in the universe, both visible and invisible, is made of this energy. It is also known as *life force*. It is the energy that creates and animates, as well as the energy that gives life.

When this energy is left unharnessed, it remains passive and simply follows the natural flow of the universe. However, in the hands of a skillful magical practitioner, this energy can be used for various purposes. It can be used to heal, motivate, inspire, and even regenerate, among others. However, it can also be used to curse, vex, and even kill. It has no limitations except only the limitations that you have placed on your mind. But, if you are able to free the mind, then this life force energy would be infinite and limitless.

But how do you make use of this energy? The answer lies in the very basics of magic which teach that all true and genuine magic starts and ends in the mind. Yes, with your mind, you can harness life force energy. It is just a matter of learning how to use the mind in a magical way.

When it comes to using the mind in a magical way, the secret lies in the use of the imagination. Interestingly, the word *imagination* is actually a confession of the identity of a magus:

i-mage or *i-mage-nation*. Imagination is the place of pure magic and witchcraft. If you want to experience a magical life, then you must learn to use your imagination in a magical way. The good news is that this is actually easy to do. Later in this book, you will learn various techniques that will allow you to put your imagination into real magical use.

It is also important to note that magical energy does not die. It cannot be destroyed. It only keeps transforming and transforming without end. All things are literally made of this energy. It also follows that once you learn how to control this energy, you will also have control over all things. Spells and rituals depend on how well you can harness this energy to bring about the change that you seek. Master this energy, and you shall be the master of the universe.

Energy Breathing Technique

Breath is life. In fact, a whole system has been developed in yoga known as *pranayama*, which specializes in the art of breathing. To breathe is life; and where there is breath, there is power.

The technique that you are about to learn uses the breath to draw energy into yourself. It is an easy and effective technique that you can use anywhere. This technique will also allow you to use the imagination in a magical way, and it will also develop your overall magical faculties. Here are the steps:

Assume a comfortable position and relax. You can do this technique in any position, even while standing or even while moving. The important thing is to keep the mind calm and relaxed.

Now, imagine magical energy all around you. You may visualize magical energy in any way that you like. It is recommended to imagine life force energy as pure white light. See and feel this energy all around you.

Breathe gently through your nose. As you do so, see and feel that you are not only breathing in air; but that together with the air, you are also breathing in life force energy. See and feel as the life force energy enters your body and your whole being. Feel the life force energy empowering you. It is also good to imagine yourself shining brighter and brighter the more that you absorb energy into yourself. Continue for as long as you like or until you are fully charged with magical energy.

Another thing that you can do with this technique is to remove all negativity from your body and soul. As you exhale, see and feel that you are not only breathing out air; but that together with the air, you are also breathing out all negative energies and all negativity from your soul. You may visualize the negative energy as some kind of black or gray smoke.

Continue the breathing cycle of inhaling fresh magical energy and exhaling negative energy. Breath, relax, and let go.

If you are a beginner, the recommended number of breaths per session is only seven breaths. You can then increase the number of breaths as you gain more experience.

Energy Quality

Life force energy can be charged with a specific quality. For example, you can charge it with the quality of healing. Once energy is charged with healing quality, the said energy can now be used for healing.

For example, in the energy breathing technique that we have just discussed, you can charge it with a specific quality that you want. With the use of the imaginative power, energy can be charged with any quality that you desire.

Let us say that you want to absorb healing energy. See and feel that the energy that you are breathing in is charged with a powerful healing force. It heals everything that it touches. See and feel the healing energy as you fill yourself with this life force.

Again, you are not limited to healing energy. If you are feeling afraid, you can imagine breathing in and absorbing the energy of courage. Feel free to charge the energy with any quality that you like.

Just because an energy is charged with a specific quality does not always mean that it will be enough. The intensity of the energy that is charged should also be considered. To make it powerful and effective, the energy must be concentrated. Keep it intact. This is something that can be developed through regular practice. Having said that, let us now move on to our next subject.

The Elements

There are four elements in the universe: fire, water, air, and earth. All things are also made of at least one of these elements. Humans are a special kind for we are composed of all the four elements, while other beings and entities are made of at least one element but not more than three.

It must be emphasized as early as now that these elements mean so much more than their mere physical representations. Hence, the fire element is not limited to the mere physical fire as we know it; the water element is not limited to the sea and the oceans, and so on. The same principle applies to the other elements (air and earth).

Every element possesses certain qualities and attributes. Let us take a closer look at them one by one:

Fire

- Flame
- Heat
- Red
- Electric
- War
- Courage
- Lust

- Willpower

- Desire

- Anger

- Passion

- Intimacy

- Romance

- Salamanders

- South direction

Water

- Oceans, seas, and all bodies of water

- West direction

- Blue

- Emotion

- Magnetic

- Healing

- Cleansing

- Mermaids and undines

- Beauty

Air

- Movement
- Travel
- East direction
- Creative communication
- Sylphs
- Levitation
- Birds and all winged-creatures
- Lightness
- Yellow
- Breath
- Feather

Earth

- North direction
- Foundation
- Stability
- Being centered and grounded
- Planet Earth

- Trees and nature

- Green and/or brown

- Survival

- Human instinct

- Healing (also has healing quality like the water element)

- manifestation

It should be noted that the said qualities and attributes of the elements are just their general characteristics. It is still up to the magus to get to know the elements and have a good relationship with them.

You must understand that the elements are very much alive. They are pure spirit forms, and they possess much magic. The key is not to force the elements to do what you want, but to establish a good bond with them.

You may feel like you feel closer toward a particular element than the others, and this is normal. However, as a magical practitioner, you must gain mastery over all the elements.

Get to Know the Elements

As a magical practitioner, it is your job to take the effort to get to know the elements. Do not worry; this is easy to do. Getting to know the elements is just about spending time with them and being open to them. It is good to take your time and get to know them one by one.

The good news is that the elements have their existence and presence in the physical plane, which makes it very easy to connect with them. So, for example, let us say that you want to get to know and connect with the element of earth, then the best way to do this is by going to nature or anywhere where you can connect with its energy. You can also stand or sit close to a tree. Some practitioners even hug a tree. You can also hold a stone or flower in your hand, knowing that it is of the earth, as you open up to its energy.

If you want to connect to the energy of the fire element, it helps so much to have the sunlight touch your body as you become conscious of its energy, knowing well that the Sun belongs to the fire element. Another thing that you can do is to light a candle and gently focus on its flame. This will naturally and automatically create a connection between you and the flame (fire element).

If you want to connect to the air element, you can go outside and enjoy the fresh air. As you inhale, feel the air energy being absorbed by your body and being. Another technique is to close your eyes and simply imagine yourself floating in the sky.

If you want to connect with the water element, you can take a bath and actually feel the water touching your skin. It is also a good practice to bathe in the sea or in a tub as you open up to the water element.

The key is to take the effort to actually spend time and connect with the energy of the elements. By doing this regularly, you will not only have a better understanding of the elements, but you will also be able to develop a good relationship with the elements even to the point where they will be glad and eager to help you in your magical work, whatever it may be.

Touch the Earth

To touch the Earth means to connect with Mother Earth on a deep and personal level. This practice is also known as *grounding*. It is considered a basic skill in witchcraft, and yet only a few practitioners are able to do it properly. This technique will also help you to significantly develop your magical faculties, especially the power of imagination and the ability to manipulate magical energy.

It is recommended to do this technique in a standing position, but this can also be done in a sitting position as long as you can have your feet flat on the ground, thereby connecting you to Mother Earth. Having said that, here are the steps:

Be comfortable and relax. Feel the Earth beneath your feet. Know that since you have been into this world, you have always been swimming in the fresh green energy of the Earth. You are of the Earth, and she takes good care of you. Indeed, Mother Earth is very much alive, and she holds various secrets of magic.

Now, see and feel that roots like those of a tree are slowly coming out from the soles of your feet. These roots are made of your own personal energy. Send them down as far as they can go deep into the Earth. Soon enough, they will hit a point where they shall stop; when this happens, just allow them to stop. Hold your position and appreciate this new-found and intimate connection that you now have with the Earth.

While you are connected to the Earth, keep your mind open. It is not uncommon for the Earth to communicate to those who connect with her on a deep level such as this one. Needless to say, the Earth usually communicates by means of telepathy, so just keep your mind open, so that you will know if Mother Earth is sharing anything with you.

Many times, simply having this connection with the Earth alone is already more than enough. However, if you want to take this technique a step further, you can also drink the fresh green energy of the Earth. As you can see, you have transformed yourself into a magical tree, with your roots deep down in Mother Earth.

To absorb the fresh green energy of the Earth, inhale—and as you inhale, see and feel that you are drinking and absorbing the green energy of the Earth through your roots. Let the energy pass through your roots, through the soles of your feet, and then into your body and being. Let every inhalation be a way of absorbing the fresh green energy of the Earth. Continue this magical breathing of absorption for as long as you like or until you are fully charged with the energy of Mother Earth.

You can end this technique at any time by thanking Mother Earth, and then gently returning to your body. To return to the body, gently bring your awareness back to your physical body, slowly move your fingers and toes, and then very gently open your eyes with a smile. Know that you can always return to the deep connection that you just had with the Earth at any time and as often as you like. The Earth is very much alive, and you walk and live in her energy.

Energy Ball

Creating an energy ball is fun, and it is also an effective way to develop your magical abilities, especially the ability to manipulate magical energy, which is very important in the magical arts. Making an energy ball is easy as long as you know how to do it properly.

As the name implies, an energy ball is a ball that is made of pure life force energy. It is a versatile tool that should be in the arsenal of a true magical practitioner. Here are the steps:

Assume a comfortable position and relax. Position your hands as if you were holding a ball, palms facing each other. Now, imagine magical energy all around you. You may visualize magical energy in any way that you want. I usually advise my students to imagine it as pure white light.

Next, see and feel that you are drawing this magical energy from the universe and have it form into a ball of energy between your hands. This is your energy ball. Continue to pour energy into this ball to make it powerful. Be sure to keep the energy concentrated and intact within the ball. This is the way to make your energy ball (as well as any other energy construct) very strong. Spend as much time as you may need to charge your energy ball with as much life force as you can.

You should be able to feel your energy ball between your hands. The sensations may vary but usually manifest as some kind of heat, pressure, gentle warmth, and/or a tingling sensation. It is also possible that you might physically see waves or a blurry spot at the location where your energy ball is. Do not force anything to happen; but instead, just keep your mind open.

After creating an energy ball, you can play around with it for a while. When you are done, you can just toss it into the air and let it disappear.

Now that you know how to make an energy ball, let us discuss how you can use it for practical purposes.

Programming Your Energy Ball

Programming an energy ball is all about giving a specific command to your energy ball. This is where you tell your energy ball what you want it to do for you.

There are two ways to program an energy ball: verbally and through the mind. Let us first discuss how you can program your energy ball by using a verbal command. This is as easy as telling your energy ball what it shall do for you. However, you should follow the same rules as when making an affirmation. The rules are as follows:

- Keep it short and simple.

- Use the present tense.

- Believe in whatever it is that you are affirming.

- Use the power of repetition.

Let us say, for example, you want to use your energy ball for healing, you can say the following affirmation: "You heal me," or "You heal me continuously." Feel free to come up with your own direct and simple affirmation. Be sure to say your affirmation at least three times. This is to further impress upon your energy ball whatever it is that you are commanding it to do. Once you feel that your desire has been impressed upon your energy ball, you can toss your energy ball away to allow it to do its task.

Another method of programming is with the use of the imagination alone. Instead of telling your energy ball what you want it to do for you, you are going to imagine your energy ball already doing its task right now. See your energy ball already performing its task repeatedly in your mind. Continue this for as long as necessary until you feel that your energy ball has already absorbed the task that you have given to it. After which, you can simply toss your energy ball into the air as a sign that you are now sending it to the universe for it to perform its task for the complete manifestation of your will.

As a true magical practitioner, you are hereby encouraged not only to use a single method of programming, but that you should apply both methods at the same time. Hence, as you give the verbal command, you should also imagine your energy ball already performing its task. This is the most effective way of programming, and this is the way of the true magus.

Bubble Shield

If you engage in the magical arts, you should also learn how to defend yourself from psychic attacks and negative energies. In some occult schools and traditions, this is a part of basic training. The good news is that it is easy to cast a defensive magic as long as you know how to do it properly.

The technique that you are about to learn is a favorite even among advanced practitioners. The reason for this is that it is a basic technique whose power lies in the skills of the caster. Therefore, the more that you grow magically and spiritually, the more powerful this shield is also going to be. Having said that, here are the steps:

Be comfortable and relax. You may close your eyes, if you want, but it is not necessary to do so. Imagine magical energy all around you. Again, visualizing the universal energy as white light is recommended.

Next, see and feel that you are drawing the universal energy toward you and have it form into a shield like a bubble around you. Know that this is your bubble shield, and it protects you from all psychic attacks and from all negative energies.

The next step is to make your bubble shield strong and powerful so as to increase its effectiveness. The way to do this is by pouring more energy into it. To do this, continue drawing energy from the universe and keep pouring it into your bubble shield. As you are doing this, you should be able to see (in your imagination) your shield shining brighter and brighter. You should also be able to feel the power of your shield as it gets stronger and stronger. Take as much time as you may need. Do not rush this part of the process. On average, this usually takes about two minutes, but some practitioners even spend as much as five to ten minutes. There are no strict rules, so just be sure to charge your bubble shield with as much energy as it can contain. Keep the energy concentrated and intact. You should be able to see and feel your bubble shield coming to life at this point.

Once you are happy with the power of your shield, you can stop pouring energy into it. You can now conclude the technique by saying an affirmation to further impress upon your shield its task, such as by telling your shield, "You protect me from all negative energies and psychic attacks."

Now that your shield is cast, you can now go about your day knowing that you have a bubble shield that protects you.

It should be noted that psychic shields require energy for them to continuously exist and perform their functions. On average, a shield created in the manner as described would last for about seven hours, depending on how much negative energies it is exposed to. However, as you gain more experience and develop your skills, the lifespan of your shield will also increase.

You are free to cast the bubble shield as often as you like. It is recommended to use it when you know that you will be exposed to various people or whenever you find yourself in a difficult situation. Once you get used to casting this shield, you can easily cast it quickly at any time, and even in public without being noticed by anyone.

Mental Projection

Mental projection is the psychic ability to project the mind, which allows you to travel the universe, including the invisible realms. It is much easier than astral projection but can be just as effective once you gain more experience. It is an excellent technique for beginners, and it is also easy to do.

Mental projection will allow you to go to whatever place that you desire in an instant. And, a good thing about this technique is that you will not be limited to the physical plane, but you can also discover the various magical realms out there. Still, if you are starting out, it is good to begin exploring the places that you are already familiar with, such as your home and neighborhood. Having said that, here are the steps:

It is good to do this technique while lying down, but just be careful not to fall completely asleep. The body should be as relaxed as possible and even be put to sleep, but the mind must stay aware and conscious of everything.

Close your eyes and free the mind. You might want to meditate for a few minutes to help prepare the mind for magical work.

With eyes closed, imagine the room where you are in. See and feel that you are looking around you with the eyes of the soul. You should be able to see the room as clearly as you can. Know that you are not looking with your physical eyes, for your physical eyes are closed, but you are now seeing with the eyes of magic — the eyes of the mind.

Next, see and feel that you are slowly rising from your body. Float a few inches above your body and look at your physical body. You can also move around the room and get comfortable with this new state of being — this is your mind being projected outside of your body. You may or may not see your mental body, and that is okay. The important thing is that you can move around outside of your body.

Although not necessary, if you want to assume a particular form, simply imagine yourself taking that form, and you shall instantly be transformed into it. This is how easy it is in the magical realm. Only the physical plane is too limiting when it comes to matters of form and shapes.

Once you have explored the room, you are free to move out and explore other places. You can move around as you normally do, but know that you are no longer limited to time and space, so you can simply imagine the place where you want to go, and you shall be transported there instantly. Such is one of the wonderful powers of the mind.

You can also go to a place that you have not yet seen. To do this, simply think of the place where you want to go, and then use your willpower to be transported to that place. By doing so, your mind will be projected to that place immediately, and you shall appear in that place at once. When you use this technique, be sure to keep an open mind. Do not force yourself to see anything. Instead. Just keep an open mind and allow everything to take their natural form and manifestation.

You can return to your body at any time. To do this, simply think of your physical body. However, do not return to your body directly right away, except if you have only projected within the same room as where your physical body is. But, if you are coming from far away, return to the room first where your body is. The reason for this is that returning to your physical body immediately from far away may cause a shock or a headache. To avoid this, return to the room first, and then once you are back in the room and can see your physical body, only then should you return into your body by sliding into it.

Mental projection will allow you to project your mind anywhere in the universe. It will also allow you to access the magical realms. The key is to keep your mind open. The more that you practice this technique, the more effective it will be. It is good to practice this technique before you sleep at night, but any time of the day or night will also be fine. It is safe to practice this technique as many times as you want and as often as you like.

Dancing Flame

The dancing flame technique is a classic of magic. It is a magical technique that will allow you to control the flame of a candle with your mind. It is a good exercise in training the mind, developing your concentration and willpower, as well as in improving your skills at telekinesis (the psychic art of moving objects with the mind). Here are the steps:

Assume a comfortable position and relax. For this exercise, you are going to need a candle. Light the candle and gently focus on the flame. Clear your mind and just stare gently at the flame of the candle.

As you focus on the candle, an instant connection will be automatically created between you and the flame. The flame is an element of fire, and it is alive. Every flame has a living spirit. Connect with this life within the flame. Be one with it. Soon enough, you will feel as though the flame is a part of yourself—like an extension of who you are, like another part of your body. Once you reach this point, imagine the flame of the candle bending to the direction that you want. You can also change the size of the flame by making it smaller or bigger. As you are doing this, also use your willpower gently. If done correctly, the flame shall move/respond in accordance with your will.

The key to significantly increasing your chances of success is to establish a strong connection with the flame. This connection will be automatically created once you focus gently on the flame.

As you are focusing on the flame, be open, and connect with it as much as you can. It is impossible to explain this through words, but you should be able to feel it as your spirit connects with the spirit of the fire element.

A word should be said about using willpower in telekinesis. There are two schools of thought on this matter. One school of thought teaches that you can impose your willpower using force. The other school of thought teaches that force must not be used, but harmony. Therefore, the connection of oneness is essential. Whether you would want to follow the first or second school of thought would be left to your own personal experimentation and preference.

Inner Light Meditation

This is a meditation technique that triggers mental projection. If you find it difficult to project your mind to a particular place, then this technique might be useful for you. The inner light meditation uses the light within you as a portal to access the otherworldly dimensions. However, unlike the previous technique which allows you to choose a particular place to go, the inner light meditation will lead you to a seemingly random place—but it is not completely random. Rather, it is a place where the universe wants to take you and wants you to see. The key here is to keep an open mind and just relax. Allow the magic of the universe to unfold right before you. Having said that, the steps are as follows:

Be comfortable and relax. Close your eyes and clear your mind. With your eyes closed, consider everything that you see that is not black as light. This is your inner light. Gently focus on this inner light.

If thoughts arise in the mind, ignore them. Only focus on the light within you. Be one with this inner light. Soon enough, and without forcing it, images and visions may start to appear. When this happens, focus on the images/visions. Gently shift your focus from the light into the images and/or visions. As this happens, relax and do not get excited. Having a strong emotion during this journey may pull you back to your body. This is a normal defense mechanism of the body to make sure that you are safe. Therefore, just relax and let go of everything. Trust in the light that shines within you, for it is your inner light—and it is the light that always connects you to Divinity.

Just relax and follow the images and visions as they unfold right before you. This is the magic of the universe revealing itself to you. Let go of everything and enjoy this magical experience.

At any time that you want to end this meditation, gently bring your awareness back to your body, slowly move your fingers and toes, and very gently open your eyes with a smile.

The more that you practice this technique, the more that you will be able to free your mind and access higher dimensions of existence. Always remember that practice makes perfect. Let the light within you guide you and reveal to you the mysteries of magic and the universe.

Magical Health

One's health is also important in living a magical life. You must understand that your physical body and your spiritual body are connected. In fact, various occult research works have shown that before any disease manifests on the physical body, it first has a manifestation on the spiritual/astral body. It then follows that by keeping your spiritual body pure and healthy through the practice of meditation and others, you can also keep the physical body healthy. In the same way, what is good for the physical body is also good for the spiritual/astral body. In fact, doing a simple physical exercise like walking can help cleanse the aura and give you a more vibrant energy.

As a magical practitioner, it is good to give attention to your health, and that you should make sure to live a healthy lifestyle. Do not worry, you do not need to engage in any strict and difficult diet. Eating healthy and living healthy would be enough. Daily exercise is also recommended. You do not need to do a heavy workout; you do not even have to go to the gym. Even light exercises like walking or doing a few jumping jacks would be fine.

By keeping your physical body healthy, you also get to keep your spiritual body healthy, and vice versa. You do not need to be a professional to do this nor do you need to work with a professional. It is as simple as eating healthy and living healthy.

Now, in our modern world, it is very easy to be in a position where you just get too busy and be always bombarded with lots of things to do, as well as stress and pressures to deal with. It is strongly recommended to keep your life as simple as possible. This way, you can have more peace of mind, and you will have more time to focus on what is really important to you.

Drawing Down the Moon

The magical practice of drawing down the Moon has been in existence since ancient times. It also has various variations. This technique will allow you to draw and absorb the energy of the Moon.

The energy of the Moon is associated with healing, peacefulness, serenity, gentleness, self-empowerment, and magic. By drawing down the Moon, you will be able to absorb her energy into yourself, thereby charging you with Moon power. The steps are as follows:

Assume a comfortable position and relax. It is good to do this technique at night where you can see the Moon in the sky. However, if this is not possible, you can still use this technique at any time, even during daylight. After all, the Moon is always up there, even when you do not see her with your eyes.

If you do not see the Moon physically for whatever reason, you can simply close your eyes and imagine the Moon above you. If you can see the Moon physically, then you can face the Moon and see and feel her light shining down on you.

See and feel that you are absorbing the energy of the Moon. To do this, inhale—and as you inhale, imagine that you are also absorbing the fresh energy of the Moon. Let every inhalation be a way to fill your body and entire being with Moon energy.

Continue absorbing the energy of the Moon for as long as necessary. When you are done, you can thank the Moon either telepathically or by saying your message of thanks out loud. You can then stop drawing energy and simply go about your day/ night knowing that you are now charged with Moon power.

42

Magical Bath

The magical bath is a form of cleansing technique. It will get rid of negative energies that may have attached themselves to you, as well as all the stresses of daily life. Simply put, it is a technique to be free from negativity. Another good thing about this technique is that you can incorporate it in your daily shower/bath. The steps are as follows:

As you are taking a bath, see and feel that you are not only removing the physical dirt from your body; but that together with the dirt, you are also removing all negative energies from your body, as well as from your being. You may visualize the negative energy as some kind of black or gray substance. See and feel that you are cleansing both your body and soul. Visualize the negative energies going down the drain. Continue to cleanse yourself until you are completely cleansed and refreshed.

This technique has a simplified variation which you can easily incorporate every time you wash your hands.The principle remains the same, except that you are not washing your whole body. In this case, see and feel all negativity from your body and being washed away as you wash your hands. Allow all the negativity to leave your body and soul through your hands. Be cleansed, body and soul.

Wish Bird

The wish bird is an effective way to manifest your desires. It is a way to communicate your desire to the universe, and for the universe to act on it, thereby bringing it to full manifestation.

It is recommended to use this magic in the morning and/or just before you sleep. But, you are still free to cast this magic at any time and even as many times as you want.

It should be noted that a wish bird is an extension of the magician/witch. It does not have a completely separate and independent existence. After all, it is also charged with your own life force, and it possesses your desire. Having said that, here are the steps:

Assume a comfortable position and relax. Clear your mind. You may close your eyes, if you want. Position your hands as if you were holding a bird. Next, imagine pulling energy from the universe and accumulating that energy in the space between your hands. See and feel that the energy is forming a bird between your hands. You are free to make your wish bird look like anything you want. Many practitioners use a white dove or an eagle, but you are free to make the bird as anything you want.

The next step is to charge your wish bird with more energy to make it powerful and effective. To do this, continue to pull energy from the universe and pour that energy into your wish bird, thereby making your wish bird stronger and stronger.

Once you are satisfied with the power of your wish bird, the next step is to impress your wish upon it. To do this, simply follow the steps on programming an energy ball.

After programming your wish bird, the next step is to charge your wish bird with your own personal life force. This is very easy to do: Simply blow upon your wish bird three times. Your breaths will automatically charge your wish bird with your personal life energy.

After the aforesaid steps, you can now send your wish bird out into the universe for the manifestation of your desire. To do this, just toss your wish bird out into the air and let it fly away. Know that your wish bird is now going to communicate your desire/ wish to the universe and bring about the change that you want.

Best Practices

Let us now discuss the essential best practices that you can observe to increase your chances of success:

Make the practice of meditation a priority

Meditation is very important if you want to have any real and serious progress in the magical arts. It is your responsibility to prioritize it. In our modern world, it is very easy to be misdirected and get too busy that you will not have the time to meditate. Never allow this modern world to manipulate you. As a true magical practitioner, you must prioritize not only the practice of meditation, but your overall magical and spiritual practices. I have met so many people who claim to be practitioners of magic but could barely cast a decent energy ball. It is a shame to claim yourself as a magical practitioner when you do not even live a magical life. From now on, be sure to prioritize your magical and spiritual life, especially the practice of meditation.

Relax

When you are manipulating magical energy, you should relax as much as you can. Effective manipulation of energy does not rely on force, but harmony. Instead of using force, you must have peace of mind, and you should let the energy flow naturally like the waters of a flowing river. Do not forget that magic is harmony with nature, not against it.

Witchcraft as a way of life

Witchcraft is a way of life. The best way of magical practice is to apply the teachings and practices as a way of life. It is disappointing to meet someone who claims to be a magical practitioner who does not even live a magical life. Real witchcraft/magic ought to be lived and experienced on a deep and personal level. Know who you really are, and never forget who you truly are. Live magically.

Keep a magic journal

Although not necessary, keeping a journal might also be helpful as it will allow you to record your development, as well as view yourself from a different and fresh perspective. You can write anything in your magic journal that is related to your magical practices and spiritual life. When keeping a journal, be sure to update it regularly. You might not appreciate its value in the beginning, especially when you are starting with a completely empty journal. Magical journals gain their value and importance over time. When you keep a journal, it is very important to be open and honest with yourself. Some people turn a blind eye on their weaknesses. This is not good. In fact, the more weaknesses that you identify in your journal, the more helpful it will be for you.

Use all your psychic senses

When you use your imagination to manipulate magical energy or whenever you create something, do not limit the imaginative power to just visual imagination. Real magical imagination includes all psychic senses. Hence, as much as possible, use all your psychic senses. This means that you should not only see what you imagine, but you must also feel it, even smell, hear, and taste it, if possible. Among all the psychic senses, the most important are the psychic senses of seeing and feeling. Be sure to always include these psychic senses whenever you use your magical imagination—and feel free to use your other psychic senses when they apply.

Practice with a friend

Although you practice witchcraft in solitary, it does not mean that you are completely prohibited from working magic with a friend. However, you must be very careful in choosing the friend that you would be working magic with. Be sure to only work with those who are also sincerely passionate in learning the magical arts. If possible, it is also advantageous if you work with a friend who has more magical knowledge and experience than you, so that you can learn from them. Still, the most important thing to note is to work with a friend who is really serious about learning and devoted to the Craft.

Experiment

You must not forget that magical practice is an art. Every magical practitioner is also a scientist. Feel free to experiment and exercise your creativity. It is also worth noting that you should not limit yourself to whatever you read in this book and from other magical books. Magic is an art form. You are encouraged to make changes to the instructions in this book. In fact, you are strongly encouraged to come up with your own magical techniques.

Reflect

It is a recommended practice to stop every now and then and just reflect on your magical life. You are also encouraged to ponder about the magical techniques that you know, and then come up with ways to make them even more effective and powerful. By looking within, you can discover more about yourself and also realize many important things about witchcraft. Do not worry, the universe will guide and help you.

Enjoy the Journey

Last but not least, you should also enjoy the journey. After all, the path of magic is infinite. Continue learning as you enjoy every step of the way. The practice of magic may have its challenges, but it is also supposed to be fun. Be happy. You deserve to be happy.

A Call to Christ

I hope that you have enjoyed reading this book. Our humble journey ends here. But, before I let you go, there is something that I want to share with you. I have been practicing witchcraft for more than 20 years, and I am now a follower of Jesus Christ. It is interesting to know that many witches and wizards these days are also turning to Christ for a genuine spirituality and for more magic.

Shortly after Christ was born, he was visited by the three magi, which some people these days refer to as the three wise men. Based on the original text, the word *magi* was used. The word *magi* is the plural of the word *magus*—and the word *magus* is where the word *magic* came from. Hence, Jesus was visited by three magical practitioners. The church did not want to talk about it and even tried to change the word into *wise men* or even the *three kings* as if to hide its real meaning. But, indeed, three magical practitioners came after Jesus was born.

In my life, despite all the magic and rituals that I have learned, I came to a point of complete darkness and depression. My magic could not save me. That was the time when Jesus came and rescued me. I have been serving Him since then.

I would like to ask my dear reader to kindly give Christ a chance in your life. Forget about what you think you know about Him from what you have learned from religion. You can start with a clean slate, and get to know him on your own. In this regard, I highly suggest starting out by reading the Bible. No, you do not need to read the whole Bible. You can start by reading the Book of Matthew, which also happens to be the first book in the New Testament of the Bible. This is a good way to know about the life and teachings of Jesus Christ. Do not worry, it is not a long book. In fact, I managed to finish reading it in just one sitting. Just please give it a try and see how it works for you.

Unlike other gods out there who do not care about you and would require a complicated ritual before they pay attention to you, Jesus is always with you, and He loves you. In fact, He loves you so much that He already suffered and died for you, so that you can enjoy salvation with Him in paradise.

I sincerely hope that you may give Christ a chance. He might just change your life forever.

With light and love, blessed be.

Don't miss out!

Visit the website below and you can sign up to receive emails whenever Merryl Kowalska publishes a new book. There's no charge and no obligation.

https://books2read.com/r/B-A-OMZV-CKLDC

BOOKS2READ

Connecting independent readers to independent writers.

Did you love *Solitary Witchcraft for Beginners*? Then you should read *A Guide to Acquiring an Astral Magic Wand*[1] by Merryl Kowalska!

[2]

Immersive Magic: A Guide to Acquiring an Astral Magic Wand is a magical manual that teaches how you can acquire your very own astral magic wand. The magic wand is one of the most important tools of a magus. The astral magic wand is not an ordinary wand, but it is a magic wand that exists in the astral plane. The fact that it exists in the astral dimension makes it very practical for magical workers since it will allow you to use your wand anywhere, even in public.

---

1. https://books2read.com/u/bpqeA9

2. https://books2read.com/u/bpqeA9

Acquiring an astral wand is easy as long as you know how to do it properly. This magical practice will also develop your overall magical faculties.

Immersive Magic: A Guide to Acquiring an Astral Magic Wand discusses the steps that you need to know to own an astral wand. It also reveals the magical places that you can visit to claim certain wands, including rare types of magic wands. As an added bonus, we will also discuss how you can create your very own astral magic wand.

It should be noted that this book is not only about acquiring an astral wand, but you will also learn how to make use of your mind in a magical way, as well as how you can effectively journey into the magical realms that are beyond the physical dimension, among others. Indeed, this book presents a journey, but it is up to you to take the actual steps.

Immersive Magic: A Guide to Acquiring an Astral Magic Wand is written in a simple, direct, and easy-to-follow format, so that you can easily focus on learning and experiencing the magic that has been long hidden away from prying eyes.

Are you ready to claim your very own astral wand? Are you ready to learn real magic? If yes, then welcome into this magical universe, for your magical journey shall now begin.

Also by Merryl Kowalska

Immersive Magic
A Guide to Acquiring an Astral Magic Wand
Solitary Witchcraft for Beginners